RAW MATERIAL SUPPLY IN A MULTIPOLAR WORLD

Yuan-li Wu

Foreword by
James E. Lee, President
Gulf Oil Corporation

National Strategy Information Center, Inc.
Published by
Crane, Russak & Company, New York

Raw Material Supply in a Multipolar World

Published in the United States by

Crane, Russak & Company, Inc.
52 Vanderbilt Avenue
New York, N.Y. 10017

Copyright © 1973 by
National Strategy Information Center, Inc.

Library Edition: ISBN 0-8448-0253-0
Paperbound Edition: ISBN 0-8448-0254-9
Library of Congress Catalog Number 73-89095

Printed in the United States of America

Strategy Papers No. 20

Table of Contents

Preface

Professor Yuan-li Wu, the author of the present monograph, is Professor of Economics at the University of San Francisco, and is also associated with the Hoover Institution on War, Revolution and Peace, Stanford, California. He served as Deputy Assistant Secretary of Defense (Policy, Plans, and National Security Council Affairs), 1969-70, and he has published many books and articles on problems of strategy and national defense. His short but provocative study on raw material supply is concerned primarily with the increasing strategic dependence of the United States and its major Free World allies, including Japan, on external sources of supply for a number of vital raw materials, especially metals and mineral fuels.

I am grateful to Mr. James E. Lee, President of the Gulf Oil Corporation, for his perceptive Foreword to Professor Wu's study. Mr. Lee calls particular attention to the growing energy shortage in the United States, and to the farreaching measures that would have to be taken if we are to continue to meet future energy demands primarily from domestic sources of supply.

Frank R. Barnett, *President*
National Strategy Information Center, Inc.

October 1973

vii

Foreword

James E. Lee, *President*
Gulf Oil Corporation

A continuing supply of certain raw materials, especially strategic metals and minerals, is absolutely essential to assure our national security. This fact has taken on much added significance today in view of rising nationalism around the globe and the increased dependence of the Western world, especially the United States, on imported raw materials. Professor Wu's monograph traces the flow of world trade in these strategic metals and minerals, and analyzes their vulnerability as to sources and supply routes.

There is another aspect of the raw material situation that should give added interest to Professor Wu's analysis, namely, the importance of economic power. Statesmen and economists are beginning to realize that, in the future, economic power will be just as important as military power in determining the ideologies of the emerging countries and in assuring that the peoples of the Western world continue to enjoy the freedoms we now take for granted.

In the past, we in the United States have had little concern about our economic power. We were unquestionably the greatest economic power in the world—by any standard of measure. Today, our economic power is endangered; and without economic power, it would be impossible to sustain first-rank military power. The United States is now a net importer of every strategic metal except copper, and of increasing quantities of petroleum. While our reliance on imports of these strategic metals and ores should give us some worry, the importation of rising quantities of petroleum should be a major cause for concern, for both strategic and economic reasons.

First, energy is required to refine the metallic ores into finished form suitable for use. Today, approximately 75 percent of our energy in the United States is derived from oil and gas; and even under the most optimistic projections, we still expect that in 1985, approximately 65 percent of our energy will be derived from oil and gas.

Second, the strategic metals can be stockpiled more easily than oil and gas. Today, Europe is targeting for a ninety-day stockpile of petroleum fuels. In the United States, there are no compulsory storage requirements, and stocks of petroleum normally are sufficient for only about sixty days.

Third, the most important exporters of metals in the Free World are Canada and Australia, and both could probably be relied on in the event of a confrontation between East and West. In the case of petroleum, the supplies available for export are largely concentrated in the Persian Gulf, and are not necessarily assured to the West in case of East-West confrontation. The July 7, 1973, issue of the *Economist* stated: "The thing to understand about the oil business is that it is more a political than an economic activity." And even if supplies were assured to the West, think of the vulnerability of a supply line stretching from the Persian Gulf around the Cape of Good Hope to Europe and the United States.

Fourth, our increasing dependence on imported petroleum will have a major impact on the balance of payments, already a source of serious concern. If the United States continues on the present trend, our dollar outflow for imported fuels could rise from about $2 billion in 1970 to $20 billion in 1980, and to as much as $30 billion in 1985. The magnitude of this problem is highlighted by the fact that, while total export of all goods and services was about $73 billion in

1972, there was a negative balance in US trade in goods and services of about $4.6 billion in 1972.

All of these facts lead me to propose that the United States should aim, as a basic national energy goal, to produce ninety percent of its total energy requirements from domestic sources. To accomplish this, *all* forms of available domestic energy must be developed as expeditiously as possible. To demonstrate the magnitude of the problem, let me cite some data taken from a report issued in December 1972 by the National Petroleum Council. This comprehensive report culminated a two-year study made at the request of the Department of the Interior, and in conjunction with representatives from all sectors of the energy industry. To meet ninety percent energy self-sufficiency in 1985 would require the following:

—Domestic crude oil production—a 37 percent increase over the 1970 rate.

—Domestic gas production—a 37 percent increase over the 1970 rate.

—Domestic coal production—a 176 percent increase over the 1970 rate.

—435 additional nuclear power plants, each with a capacity of one million KW.

—8 shale oil plants, each with a capacity of 100,000 barrels a day.

—13 oil-from-coal plants, each with a capacity of 50,000 barrels a day.

—30 gas-from-coal plants, each with a capacity of 250 mm SCF/D.

—19 geothermal plants, each with a capacity of one million KW.

It is worth noting that, as of today, the United States has no commercial shale oil plants, no oil-from-coal plants, no gas-from-coal plants, negligible geothermal capacity, and only 29 operating nuclear plants of an average size of only about 500,000 KW. Of the energy sources cited above, only increased coal production and increased oil and gas production—assuming accelerated and successful exploration efforts—can add materially to our energy supplies before 1980. The long lead times for installing and starting up facilities for the other sources preclude a significant contribution from them until 1982 or later. Yet such facilities must be initiated promptly if they are to be available at that time.

Although the basic technology appears to have been developed for shale oil and coal gasification, much engineering and process development remains to be done. Environmental problems must also be solved before commercialization is feasible. Acceptable solutions can be developed through the extensive capability of private industry—if there is hope of economic reward for the effort. Government can and must provide the necessary climate for implementing this effort. The technology for the production of oil from coal is at an earlier stage of development. Development of this technology should be energetically continued, since it is potentially an important long-range source of liquid hydrocarbons for transportation fuels, lubricants, and chemical feedstocks.

On a more long-range basis, a federal government-supported research effort should be initiated in such systems as geothermal energy, solar energy, magneto-hydrodynamics, nuclear fusion, fuel cells, low-lead hydroelectric power, use of agricultural and waste products for power, tidal power, wind power, ocean currents, and thermal gradient power. Other energy-related projects that could and probably should be supported by a federal government research effort include automated mining methods, *in situ* fuels conversion, cryogenic electric power transmission, and alternatives to internal combustion engines.

Finally, I would point out that for each additional million barrels per day of oil, produced as crude oil synthetically, or for every trillion cubic feet per year of gas produced domestically, either from gas wells or from synthetic sources, the nation could reduce imports by \$1.5 billion a year. Instead of being transferred abroad, this money could be used to pay for equipment, labor, and services in the United States, directly benefitting the domestic economy. In addition to this financial incentive, the establishment of a domestic synthetic fuels industry, even on a modest scale, would greatly strengthen the nation's strategic position.

1

Introduction

If certain raw materials are essential to a country's economic life and its defense capability, and if the country's domestic production lags substantially behind consumption, that country will be dependent upon imports to meet the shortfall. In this circumstance, the country in question will be interested in having (1) secure external sources of supply, (2) adequate and appropriate means of payment for the imports it requires, and (3) secure transportation for the imports en route. In wartime, an adversary could direct its attack on any one or more of these three factors underlying the security of the country's raw material supply. Even in peacetime, serious vulnerability on this score would make the country susceptible to political pressure by other nations. Hence, if a nation is unable to achieve a high degree of security in this respect except with the good will of allies or the sufferance of adversaries, it is really not qualified to act in a totally independent manner unless it is involved in some kind of alliance system with other nations that can achieve such security for themselves.

The central issue that this monograph will explore is, How will this problem affect Western Europe and Japan as the world shifts from US-Soviet bipolarity toward a multipolar international system? To put the question more bluntly: From the point of view of raw material supply, do the European members of NATO and Japan fully qualify as totally independent centers of power in an emerging multipolar world? And even if they do so now, how will their situation change in the future?

Some elaboration of the foregoing premises is called for. First, how essential a particular raw material is depends upon the technology available to a particular country at a given time. In this respect, industrial raw materials differ from food supply, which a nation can never do without. In the long run, substitutes can be found for most industrial raw materials. Hence, in assessing the strategic significance of a particular item, one must bear in mind the degree of substitutability. The same applies to given sources of supply and transportation routes.

A second point follows from the first. That is, the strategic significance of a raw material increases as the number of industries requiring it increases. Such multiplicity of use would automatically reduce substitutability unless, as discussed below, some of the end-uses are "nonessential" and can be curtailed. By the same token, the strategic value of a particular transportation route or a particular supplier country will rise as the number of raw materials that must pass over that route or can be supplied by that country increases. This "multiplicity aspect" points to the vital importance of energy resources that are needed by all sectors of production. It can also be used to identify certain raw material suppliers and routes of transportation as pivotal in the network of the world's raw material supply.

In the third place, although variations in the availability of raw materials that are used by a large number of industries can have a greater and more widespread economic effect or defense impact than other commodities, in an emergency it may be easier to curtail "nonessential" consumption in order to boost supply to the essential sectors. If domestic production is at least a significant portion of total supply, one can more readily "make do" with a smaller total supply by curtailing nonessential use in times of reduced import availability.

Finally, while security of supply is traditionally regarded as the central issue in evaluating both the strategic significance of imported raw materials and the vulnerability of specific user countries, another aspect of the problem has come to the forefront in recent years. As a result of the enormous expansion of the world economy since World War II, and the greatly increased consumption of certain raw materials, many countries producing and exporting these resources are no longer the hapless victims (as they once thought of themselves) exploited by countries importing their products. The effect of this economic change has been compounded by anticolonial sentiment and the rise of nationalism; and these, in turn, have been deliberately cultivated by a few big powers intent on altering the international status quo.

The consequences of all this are best exemplified by the nationalization of foreign mining investments and the increased royalty rates and earnings of petroleum exporting countries.[1] The latter have already accumulated large sums of foreign exchange, and they can expect to receive an increasing flow of earnings in the near future.[2] Collectively and as individual countries, they are more and more in a position to influence world events by using the wealth they command. Some could try to do so by financing illicit arms trade, which —at least for the short term—conceivably could alter regional strategic balances. Others engage in the direct incitement of insurgencies

---

[1] The Organization of Petroleum Exporting Countries (OPEC) was formed in 1960 by Iran, Iraq, Saudi Arabia, Kuwait, Abu Dhabi, Qatar, Libya, Algeria, Venezuela, and Indonesia. In 1970, they were able to force the international oil companies to break the previous practice of sharing oil revenues equally between the foreign companies and the host country governments. "Posted prices" on which taxes are based, as well as the tax rates, have both been raised. See, for example, the section on oil in *Strategic Survey 1970* (London: Institute for Strategic Studies, 1971). See also the series by Juan de Onis in *New York Times*, April 16, 1973.
    In contrast to oil price, the prices of metals showed divergent patterns of fluctuation during the late 1960s and 1970-71. See United Nations, *Monthly Bulletin of Statistics*, vol. 27, no. 1 (January 1973), Table 59, pp. 174-175.

[2] US estimates have put the oil revenues of the Arab countries at less than $5 billion in 1970, but have projected their rise to $40 billion a year by 1980. These figures should not be confused with the accumulated foreign exchange holdings they now have on hand. See the report on "Oil Diplomacy" by Robert Keatley in *Wall Street Journal*, January 30, 1973.

and local wars.[3] Still others could exert a destabilizing influence on the world monetary system by shifting their large foreign assets from one currency or one country to another, if for no other reason than considerations of pecuniary interest.

Thus, a new dimension has been added to the strategic significance of raw material supply. While securing an essential raw material supply by the principal user countries, or conversely, attempting to deny such security of supply by their adversaries, remain the central issues, the attitude of important raw material supplier countries must now be examined more carefully. Some of the supplier countries are no longer pawns in the strategic maneuvers of the great powers. They have become actors in their own right. And unfortunately, their behavior may be highly unpredictable.

Metals and Other Key Raw Materials

Since the number of raw materials that enter world trade is very large, an attempt must be made to select a few items for discussion within the space available. A clue to the most important of them can be found by examining certain statistics of raw material trade. According to a recent issue of the *Minerals Yearbook* of the US Bureau of Mines, 51.4 percent of the world's trade in minerals in 1968 consisted of metals, while 44.5 percent was accounted for by mineral fuels. Within the metals sector, about four fifths of the trade were made up by (1) iron and steel, and (2) nonferrous metals. Accordingly, for practical purposes we can focus our attention on mineral fuels and certain metals in the ferrous and nonferrous sectors, while we can safely disregard the "nonmetals."

---

[3] An Associated Press report from London on the seizure of an arms shipment destined for the IRA off the Irish coast mentioned the possibility that the arms had been loaded in Tripoli, Libya. (Reported in the *San Francisco Examiner*, April 3, 1973). Sporadic reports of this nature also circulated during 1972 about arms shipments received by insurgents in the Philippines.

A United Press report from Beirut on April 15, 1973, quoted Qadhafi as saying: "Libya is extending assistance to several peoples fighting for their freedom in Northrn Ireland, the Philippines, the heart of Africa, and the two Americas." (Quoted in the *San Francisco Examiner*, April 16, 1973.)

TABLE 1

Percent Distribution of World Trade in Minerals
1968

	Export Value
Metals	51.4
All ores, concentrates, and scrap	10.8
Iron and steel	22.2
Nonferrous metals	18.4
Nonmetals	4.1
Mineral fuels	44.5
Total	100.0

Source: Bureau of Mines, US Department of the Interior, *Minerals Yearbook 1969,* vol. 4, Table 4, p. 24.

Metals in World Trade and in the Engineering Industry

Among the metals, some effort to rank the individual items must be made. This can be done on the basis of different criteria. First, in terms of total value of output, the first fifteen most important metallic ores and concentrates, arranged in descending order, are (1) iron, (2) copper, (3) aluminum, (4) manganese, (5) magnesium, (6) zinc, (7) mercury, (8) lead, (9) nickel, (10) tin, (11) potassium, (12) uranium, (13) silver, (14) beryllium, and (15) gold.[4]

Second, as an indicator of bulk, an important consideration in handling, transportation, and processing, the same items can be

---

[4] See Charles L. Kimbell, "Minerals in the World Economy," in Bureau of Mines, US Department of Interior, *Minerals Yearbook 1969*; and K. P. Wang, "Minerals and Metals in International Trade," a lecture given at a UN Interregional Seminar on Mineral Economics held at Ankara, Turkey, in October 1970. We are examining here only the primary items, that is, ores and concentrates, rather than semiprocessed and fabricated products, such as steel.

ranked according to annual production by weight. On this basis, the first fifteen in descending order are (1) iron, (2) manganese, (3) sodium, (4) aluminum, (5) chromium, (6) copper, (7) zinc, (8) lead, (9) potassium, (10) nickel, (11) zirconium, (12) lithium, (13) tin, (14) magnesium, and (15) antimony.[5]

Third, since we are interested in the network of raw material trade between countries, we should also rank the principal metals in world trade by both weight and value. Use of these indicators will give us some idea about the demand on shipping for the movement of individual items and their relative economic importance to the trading nations. On this basis, the first eight metallic ores in international trade in 1968, in descending order of weight, are (1) iron ore, (2) bauxite, (3) manganese, (4) zinc, (5) copper, (6) lead, (7) nickel, and (8) tin.[6] Of the eight, only 350,000 tons of nickel and 170,000 tons of tin entered world trade in 1968. In contrast, 1.5 million tons of lead, the sixth item (including both ore and refined lead) were traded. In terms of value in world trade, the order would be (1) iron ore, (2) alumina and bauxite, (3) nickel, (4) zinc ore, (5) tin, (6) manganese ore, (7) lead ore, and (8) tungsten in ore.

Fourth, while the first two criteria offer a general indication of the relative importance of the different metals in industrial production as a whole, and the third criterion presents an index of their relative significance in world trade, we need a separate criterion for evaluation from the point of view of specific uses. For this purpose, we can direct our attention to the engineering industry, which is especially important for defense. In this respect, according to Fisher, the most important metals with major applications in engineering are (1) iron, (2) aluminum, (3) copper, (4) lead, (5) zinc, (6) manganese, (7) chromium, (8) nickel, (9) magnesium, and (10) tin.[7]

A careful scrutiny of the above schemes of ranking leads to a very

[5] *Ibid.*
[6] *Ibid.*
[7] Frank L. Fisher, *Classification of Metals, Their Etymology and Functional Grouping,* (Washington: Bureau of Mines, October 1965).

interesting construction. Since we are primarily concerned with the flow of significant raw materials among countries, we might begin with the six most important metals in world trade by weight as well as value. Leaving out nickel and tin, which do not require too much shipping because of the relatively low weight of the quantities traded, the most important items seem to be iron ore, bauxite, manganese, zinc, copper, and lead. The same six are also the most important six items among the ten metals that have major applications in engineering. Furthermore, these six items are among the first eight of the fifteen metals ranked by production value and by total weight in production. Since data on manganese are not readily available for all the countries we wish to consider, we shall treat only five of the above items—iron ore, copper, lead, zinc, and bauxite—as the principal metals to be considered in this paper. These five metals also happen to be the most common ferrous and nonferrous metals. In addition, we shall consider petroleum, the principal mineral fuel, and uranium, the basic raw material of nuclear weapons, as among the key raw materials whose supply should be discussed from the strategic point of view.

2

Metals, Oil, and the Major Powers

Principal Exporting and Importing Countries of Metals

The principal exporting and importing countries of the selected metals, as well as some others, that are important for the engineering industries can be readily identified from statistics of world trade by commodity. The following lists of principal exporting and importing countries, grouped by geographical region, provides some basic information for further analysis. The geographical division serves as a reminder that transportation routes are determined by the locations of both the exporter and the importer.

On the export side, several Latin American countries export one or more of the metallic ores on our list in significant quantities. Surinam and Guyana are major exporters of bauxite and alumina.

Chile and Peru are principal exporters of copper. Peru is also a large supplier of lead and zinc; Brazil, of manganese; and Bolivia, of tin. In addition, Mexico is a significant supplier of lead; and Jamaica, of bauxite.

In Africa, Zambia (East Africa) is a prinicipal supplier of copper; Zaire supplies both copper and zinc; and the Union of South Africa and Gabon (West Africa) are major suppliers of manganese. Liberia, Mauritania, and Sierra Leone, all in West Africa, are important exporters of iron ore.

In South Asia, India is a large exporter of iron ore and manganese. In Southeast Asia, Indonesia, Malaysia, and Thailand are major exporters of tin, while the Philippines is an exporter of copper.

Above all, however, the most important exporters of metals in the Free World are probably Canada and Australia. Canada is a source of iron, nickel, copper, lead, zinc, and aluminum; Australia exports large quantities of iron, manganese, lead, zinc, and aluminum. In terms of numbers of different metallic ores exported, Peru and India follow Canada and Australia at a distance.

Among the Communist countries, the USSR is an important exporter of five of the six most important metals on our list, including iron ore, manganese, lead, zinc, and aluminum. Hungary, Yugoslavia, and Poland each export one or more of the six metals. The People's Republic of China is traditionally an exporter of tin, tungsten, and antimony.

On the import side of eight metals (the basic six plus nickel and tin), West Germany and the United Kingdom are important importers of all eight; and France, of seven (except iron ore). On the other side of the world, Japan is a principal importer of all eight, although it produces some low grade manganese. The United States is a large importer of seven of the eight items (excluding copper, which it exports). None of the European Communist countries is a major importer of these items from outside the Communist system. The PRC is a large importer of copper.

Even this cursory examination suffices to show that both the principal European partners of NATO and Japan are major importers of key metallic ores. In common with the United States, they are large importers of the group of principal metals. In contrast, neither the USSR nor its satellite countries are large importers of these items from outside the Communist system. The same is true in the case of mainland China, the major exception here being copper. Of course, the PRC does not enjoy the same degree of self-sufficiency in fabricated metals such as special alloy steels.

The Share of Imports in Total Supply: The West Versus the Communist Powers

Although a large import total does not necessarily imply a high degree of import dependence, the three principal European allies of the United States in NATO are, in general, highly dependent upon imports for some of the key metals. West Germany, the largest contributor to NATO ground forces, imported 68 percent of its total iron ore supply in 1968. The corresponding ratio of imports to total supply was 56 percent for the United Kingdom, but only eight percent for France. In the Pacific, 93 percent of Japan's iron ore supply in 1968 was imported.[8] In the same year, West Germany was dependent upon imports for 97 percent of its copper. The corresponding degree of dependence upon imports was a hundred percent for both the United Kingdom and France. Japan was 65 percent dependent upon imports for its copper.

In the case of lead, the ratio of imports to total supply in 1968 was 72 percent for West Germany, 93 percent for the United Kingdom, 75 percent for France, and 55 percent for Japan. The corresponding ratios in the case of zinc were 46 percent for West Germany, a hundred percent for the United Kingdom, ninety percent for France, and 61 percent for Japan. Also in 1968, West Germany, the

---

[8] Although the data are those of 1968, the degree of import dependence in the cases cited has not changed. We have used 1968 data because information on specific sources of supply and routes of transportation, to be discussed in the next section, is not fully available for later years.

United Kingdom, and Japan were all totally dependent upon imports for bauxite. France, on the other hand, derived only eleven percent of its total supply from imports.

On the whole, therefore, West Germany and the United Kingdom, the two mainstays of joint NATO defense planning in Europe, are both significantly dependent upon imported metallic ores and concentrates. The parallel between the United Kingdom in Europe and Japan in the Pacific is especially noteworthy. The United States, on the other hand, is comparatively much better off than its allies in this respect. In 1968, it imported 34 percent of its supply of iron ore, 32 percent of its copper, nineteen percent of its lead, 51 percent of its zinc, and 88 percent of its bauxite. The degree of import dependence is generally lower for the United States, and the significance of some of the high import ratios is modified further by the proximity of certain principal sources of foreign supply. (See Table 2)

The Soviet Union is in a distinctly more favorable position. It is the world's leading producer of iron ore and manganese. In 1968, it was the fourth largest producer of bauxite (after Jamaica, Australia, and Surinam);[9] Soviet output of bauxite in that year was estimated at five million metric tons, as compared to 8.5 million tons for Jamaica, 5.7 million tons for Surinam, and about four million tons for Australia. (Australia has since become the world's second largest producer of bauxite.) In the same year, the Soviet Union produced 850,000 tons of mine copper, second only to United States output of 1.1 million tons (of copper content), but larger than Zambia and Italy, each producing about 670,000 tons. In 1968, the USSR was the largest producer of mine lead at 420,000 tons, although it has since been surpassed by the United States and Australia. The Soviet Union is the second largest producer of zinc in the world, although lagging behind Canada by a large margin. In 1968, Soviet zinc output was 575,000 tons, as compared to 1.2 million tons for Canada.

---

[9] The data on Soviet production and statistics are taken from Kimbell, *loc.cit.*

TABLE 2

Domestic Production and Import of Selected Metallic Ores
and Concentrates, 1968

		West Germany	
	Production	Imports	*Percent of Imports in Total Supply*
Bauxite	. . .	1,978	100
Copper (copper content)	1.32	382	97
Lead (lead content)	52.44	135.5	72
Zinc (zinc content)	117.48	100.7	46
Iron Ore	6,444	39,644	86
		United Kingdom	
Bauxite	. . .	442	100
Copper (copper content)	. . .	484	100
Lead (lead content)	3.7	49	93
Zinc (zinc content)	. . .	166.7	100
Iron Ore	13,944	17,534	56
		France	
Bauxite	2,712	335	11
Copper (copper content)	. . .	269	100
Lead (lead content)	26.4	80.4	75
Zinc (zinc content)	21.8	189.6	90
Iron Ore	55,236	5,017	8

		Japan	
Bauxite	. . .	2,450	100
Copper (copper content)	119.9	236	66
Lead (lead content)	62.9	78	55
Zinc (zinc content)	264	409.2	61
Iron Ore	5,430	68,143	93
		United States	
Bauxite	1,692	12,618	88
Copper (copper content)	1,093.2	507	32
Lead (lead content)	326.4	78.4	19
Zinc (zinc content)	480	495.7	51
Iron Ore	86,508	44,646	34

Sources: United Nations, *Monthly Bulletin of Statistics* (January 1973). Charles L. Kimbell, "Minerals in the World Economy," in Bureau of Mines, US Department of Interior, *Minerals Yearbook 1969*, vol. 4.

While Soviet production of these ores exceeds that of many ore exporting countries, because of its own large domestic consumption, Soviet exports are smaller than they might otherwise be. Nevertheless, in 1968, the Soviet Union managed to be a net exporter of iron ore and copper, according to available statistics.

Principal Importing and Exporting Countries of Crude Oil

Metals can be stored, and in general, metal products can be used repeatedly for a considerable length of time. Because of these qualities, essential metals can be stockpiled, and scrap metal can be recycled for use as raw material. On the other hand, "single-use" producer goods, such as most energy resources, do not possess these properties, at least not to the same degree. Liquid fuels and natural gas, for instance, while storable, are highly combustible. Hence, concentrations of stocks are vulnerable to enemy attack in wartime and to destruction through sabotage. Furthermore, since their usefulness disappears as soon as they are used, it is not possible to augment supply through recovery from "scrap" sources. While coal is more storable and the uranium fuel used by power reactors can last a long time, the first has given way to liquid fuels as the principal source of energy, while atomic power still accounts for only a small portion of the total energy supply.

In 1970, liquid fuels were responsible for just under fifty percent of the total energy consumption of the world's developed countries. Solid fuels were responsible for about one fourth of total consumption, only slightly larger than the share of natural gas. Hydropower and "nuclear power and imported electricity" accounted for less than three percent of the total.[10]

Among the principal European partners of NATO, both West Germany and the United Kingdom had a 1970 deficit (domestic production less consumption) of 45 percent in their consumption of energy from all sources. The corresponding deficit for France was 69 percent. In the Pacific, Japan's deficit in its energy balance was 83 percent. The United States had a nine percent deficit; and in contrast, the Soviet Union had a twelve percent surplus. (See Tables 3 and 3a.)

In order to make up its deficit, West Germany imported 151 million metric tons (in coal equivalent) of liquid fuels, while exporting 13.6 million tons of solid fuels. As can be seen from the accompanying tables, the general practice of the deficit countries is to import proportionately far more liquid fuels than solid fuels. Thus, the

---

[10] According to UN statistics, aggregate energy consumption in the developed countries amounted to 4,299.8 million metric tons of coal equivalent. Of this total, solid fuels accounted for 1,113.1 million metric tons; liquid, 2,058.7 million tons; natural and imported gas, 1,013.0 million tons; hydro and nuclear power and imported electricity, 115.0 million tons. See *World Energy Supplies, 1961-1970*, Statistical Papers, Series J, no. 15, Table 2 (New York: United Nations, 1972).

volume of liquid fuels in world trade is much greater than that of solid fuels, and crude oil is a major part of the liquid fuels imported.

The world's largest importer of crude petroleum in 1970 was Japan, followed by Italy, France, the United Kingdom, and West Germany. Together, they accounted for 587 million tons of crude oil imports, or about fifty percent of the world's total shipments of crude oil in that year.[11] Both the United Kingdom and Japan are virtually a hundred percent dependent upon imported oil. Imports in 1970 accounted for 97.5 percent of France's total crude oil supply; and the proportion was 93 percent for West Germany, and 97.1 percent for all of Western Europe.

The Soviet Union produced 352.6 million tons of crude oil in 1970, and had a net export of 64.3 million tons. The United States, on the other hand, produced 499.6 million tons of crude in the same year, but had a net import of 65.5 million tons—which happened to approximate the magnitude of the Soviet Union's net export. Communist China produced about twenty million tons of crude in 1970, and was on balance a small net exporter.[12]

On the export side, the relatively neutral or pro-Western Arab states of the Persian Gulf exported a total of 342 million metric tons of crude in 1970. Of these countries, Saudi Arabia and Kuwait supplied the largest amounts, 149 and 121 million tons, respectively. In addition, Iran, the largest single producer in the area, supplied 165 million tons; while Gabon and Nigeria in West Africa together exported about 56 million tons. In the Western Hemisphere, Venezuela exported 128 million tons, and Canada supplied 33 million. In the Pacific area, Indonesia exported 31 million tons. (See Table 4.)

These sources in the Middle East, West Africa, and the Western Hemisphere exported a total of 754 million tons of crude. If we add

---

[11] *Ibid*, Table 9, "World Movement of Crude Petroleum: 1967-1970."
[12] *Ibid*, Table 8, "Production, Trade and Apparent Supply of Crude Petroleum and Refinery Capacity." The import figures shown on this table for China are believed to refer to Taiwan's imports. Data for Taiwan have not been listed separately by the UN since the PRC's admission to the organization in October 1971.

TABLE 3

The Energy Balance of Selected Major Powers
1970
(million metric tons of coal equivalent)

	NATO		
	West Germany	*United Kingdom*	*France*
All Energy Sources			
Domestic Production	174.3	163.7	59.3
Consumption	317.0	299.1	193.0
Deficit (—) or Surplus (+)	—142.7	—135.4	—133.7
Import	187.0	160.9	161.8
Export	35.7	30.7	15.4
Net Import (—)	—151.3	—130.2	—146.4
Solid Fuels			
Consumption	130.6	152.3	55.7
Domestic Production	144.2	144.6	39.0
Net Import (—)	+13.6	—7.7	—16.7
Liquid Fuels			
Consumption	160.3	126.8	115.6
Domestic Production	9.8	0.2	3.4
Net Import (—)	—150.5	—126.6	—112.2

	Japan	*United States*	*USSR*
All Energy Sources			
Domestic Production	54.8	2,053.8	1,210.6
Consumption	332.4	2,279.0	1,076.9
Deficit (—) or Surplus (+)	—277.6	—225.2	+133.7
Import	314.2	272.9	17.0
Export	0.7	77.8	162.9
Net Import (—)	—313.5	—195.1	+145.9
Solid Fuels			
Consumption	89.4	470.7	452.1
Domestic Production	39.8	543.3	472.6
Net Import (—)	—49.6	+72.6	+20.5
Liquid Fuels			
Consumption	227.3	933.7	345.5
Domestic Production	1.0	649.5	458.3
Net Import (—)	—226.3	—284.2	+112.8

(+) = Export surplus

Source: *World Energy Supplies, 1961-1970,* UN Statistical Papers, Series J, no. 15 (New York: United Nations, 1972), Table 2.

Tunisia's export of about 3 million tons, a grand total of 757 million tons was exported in 1970 by countries that are on relatively good terms with the United States and its NATO and Japanese allies. This total amount can be compared with aggregate gross imports of 835 million tons, or net imports of 833 million tons, by the United States, Japan, and all of Western Europe. Thus, there would have been a deficiency even if the oil exports of the countries mentioned above had gone entirely to the three principal Western importing areas. The fact, of course, is that a part of the exports of the friendly producing countries was taken by other buyers, while oil from other producers had to be imported by the West.

The principal exporters we have omitted so far are Libya, Iraq, and Algeria, followed by Egypt and Syria. In 1970, the five generally anti-Western Arab states exported 296 million tons of crude (a net export of 294 million tons). Of these five, Libya and Iraq accounted for 160 million and 73 million tons respectively, or eighty percent of the total. Thus, exports from the militant Arab states was an essential factor in bridging what would otherwise have been an energy supply gap in the Western "grand alliance." As a matter of fact, some of the more militant Arab sources were by far the most important suppliers of crude to several important European NATO members, notably West Germany, France, and Italy. To complete this general picture of Western dependence for oil upon sources that are potentially hostile, attention should also be called to some 67 million tons of Soviet exports in 1970; a portion of this amount went to Western Europe.

Demand and Supply of Uranium

The general increase in demand for energy resources has caused many countries to turn to nuclear power. According to the European Nuclear Energy Agency and the International Atomic Energy Agency, the world's total nuclear generating capacity amounted to 18,000 megawatts in 1970. The principal producers were the United States and the United Kingdom, accounting for 6,100 mws and 5,300 mws, respectively. They are followed by Japan (1,800 mws), France (1,500

TABLE 3a

The Energy Balance in Western Europe
(million metric tons of coal equivalent)
1970

	EEC	Selected Countries of NATO (Excluding the United Kingdom, West Germany, and France)						All European Members of NATO (except Iceland)
		Turkey	Denmark	Norway	Portugal	Italy	Greece	
All Sources								
Domestic Production	320.582	10.947	0.048	7.623	0.995	26.391	2.863	506.708
Consumption	780.027	16.867	28.848	18.670	6.617	146.102	11.197	1,161.369
Deficit	—459.445	—5.920	—28.800	—11.047	—5.622	—119.711	—8.334	—654.661
Import	672.677	5.435	32.469	15.258	7.415	163.147	8.879	902.994
Export	159.748	0.321	3.256	2.707	0.738	36.967	0.401	197.845
Net Import (—)	—512.929	—5.114	—29.213	—12.551	—6.677	—126.180	—8.478	—705.149
Solid Fuels								
Consumption	229.558	6.259	3.715	1.506	1.257	12.673	2.953	397.504
Domestic Production	199.934	6.071	0.045	0.465	0.271	0.991	2.534	353.882
Net Import (—)	—29.624	—0.188	—3.670	—1.041	—0.986	—11.682	—0.419	—43.662
Liquid Fuels								
Consumption	445.108	10.230	25.654	10.110	4.633	107.489	7.912	630.468
Domestic Production (crude oil)	17.636	4.498	....	....	....	1.956	....	22.337
Net Import (—)	—427.472	—5.732	—25.654	—10.110	—4.633	—105.533	—7.912	—608.131

Source: *World Energy Supplies, 1961-1970,* UN Statistical Papers, Series J, no. 15 (New York: United Nations, 1972), Table 2.

TABLE 4

Crude Oil Production and Export in Major Exporting Countries
1970
(in million metric tons)

Militant Arab States	Production	Export	Import
Algeria	48.3	46.0	—
Egypt	16.4	12.9	1.0
Syria	4.2	3.5	1.2
Libya	161.7	160.2	—
Iraq	76.4	73.3	—
Other Arab States			
Kuwait	137.4	121.0	—
Qatar	17.4	17.4	—
Oman	16.6	16.6	—
Saudia Arabia	176.9	148.8	—
Union of Arab Emirates	37.9	37.9	—
Tunisia	4.1	3.2	.4
Other Countries			
Iran	191.7	165.4	—
West Africa			
Gabon	5.4	4.5	—
Nigeria	54.2	51.7	—
Venezuela	194.4	127.6	—
Canada	67.5	32.5	29.3
Indonesia	42.2	30.8	—
USSR	352.6	66.8	2.5

Source: *World Energy Supplies, 1961-1970*, UN Statistical Papers, Series J, no. 15 (New York: United Nations, 1972), Table 8.

mws), West Germany (800 mws), and, at a lower level, Spain, India, and Italy, each with 600 mws.[13] Estimates of the same sources indicate that by 1980, some ten to fifteen percent of the world's total electric generating capacity will consist of nuclear power. This would make the total nuclear generating capacity 302,600 mws, with the United States (150,00 mws) heading the list, followed by the United Kingdom (26,200 mws), West Germany (25,000 mws), Japan (23,500 mws), France (9,200 mws), Italy (8,000 mws), Canada (8,000 mws), and so on.[14] Moreover, these statistics are being constantly revised upward.[15]

The change in technology from fossil fuels to nuclear power raises the question of uranium supply and the availability of uranium enrichment facilities. As of 1970, the United States was the Free World's largest producer of uranium oxide (U_3O_8); its output for the year was 12,800 short tons. South Africa and Canada, at 4,100 and 4,000 short tons, respectively, were the second largest producers in the Free World. France produced 1,600 tons of U_3O_8 in 1970. Following at some distance were Australia, which produced 330 short tons in 1970, and Gabon in West Africa, a supplier of about 500 short tons. Other small producers in the non-Communist world included Portugal, Spain, and Sweden in Western Europe, Niger and the Malagasy Republic in Africa, and Argentina in the Western Hemisphere.

It is clear that Western Europe would have to turn to the Western Hemisphere and South Africa for uranium supplies, as well as to some West African states. In the case of Japan, the supply of uranium would have to be derived, in the main, either from across the Pacific or from Australia. The Australian production capacity can perhaps be expanded to 1,500 short tons a year by 1975.[16]

For uranium enrichment, there are at present only a few suppliers

---

[13] Quoted by Walter C. Woodmansee, "Uranium," *Minerals Yearbook 1970*, vol. 1 (Washington: Bureau of Mines, 1972), p. 1152.
[14] *Ibid.*
[15] For instance, the revised energy plan of Japan published in mid-1972 has already raised that country's goal for 1980 to 31,770 mws.
[16] See Woodmansee, *loc. cit.*

in the Free World, since the end-product could be used for the production of weapons grade uranium. France, however, has offered to construct an enrichment plant jointly with Japan.[17] In the Free World, the United States will for some time remain as the principal source of enriched uranium for the growing number of nuclear power plants. As of 1970, the main buyers of enriched uranium from the US Atomic Energy Commission were Euratom (Belgium, France, Italy, and the Netherlands), the United Kingdom, and Japan.

The demand for both uranium ore and enriched uranium would rise even further if any of the nonnuclear Free World countries should decide to develop an independent nuclear weapons capability. If so, additional sources of supply may have to be developed. Where they will be would depend upon the future of the Nuclear Nonproliferation Treaty.

In the long run, the shift toward nuclear power would not necessarily free the present large importers of energy resources from their import requirements unless the current light-metal, fast-breeder reactor program, or other similar developments, can radically change the balance between uranium supply and demand. However, this technology is still at its testing and development stage.[18] For the next several years, the uranium reactor does not offer a panacea, and atomic power can provide at best only a small portion of total energy supply. The general pattern of dependence upon imported oil by the major developed countries and allies of the United States will remain essentially unchanged, even if the potential strain on the world's tanker fleet can be reduced somewhat by conversion from oil to nuclear power.

---

[17] The French proposal to construct an enrichment plant "in the Pacific area" was reported in the *Japan Economic Journal*, vol. 9, no. 477 (July 20, 1971), p. 8. Another alternative proposed was to build the $600-1,000 million plant jointly with Australia and Japan.
[18] See "Reactor Technology," in *Annual Report to Congress of the Atomic Energy Commission for 1971* (Washington: January 1972).

3

Raw Material Supply Routes

A country importing essential raw materials from a contiguous friendly neighbor does not become vulnerable by virtue of its reliance upon imports. On the other hand, if an extended sea route is involved, the degree of vulnerability to hostile interference is increased. For example, West Germany's import of iron ore from France belongs to the first category, while its import of bauxite from Greece is in the second. On this basis, in so far as the raw material supply of the three principal European members of NATO is concerned, we can distinguish the following major sea routes: (1) the Mediterranean; (2) the Indian Ocean and the Eastern Atlantic (for exporting countries in South Asia, the Middle East, and East Africa); (3) the Eastern Atlantic, including the North Sea (for suppliers in West Africa and Scandinavia); (4) across the Indian Ocean and the Eastern Atlantic (for suppliers located east of the Malacca Strait, such as Australia); and (5) across the Atlantic (from countries in North and Latin America).

For simplicity, we shall treat shipments between the United Kingdom and Western Europe as between contiguous neighbors. Tables 5 and 6 present the detailed routing information on the supply of crude oil and selected metals to West Germany, the United Kingdom, and France. Disregarding imports between contiguous friendly countries on land, 45 percent of West Germany's total crude oil supply (domestic production plus imports) in 1968 was carried on Route One, and another 32 percent on Route Two. For iron ore during the same year, the most important shipping routes were Three (fifty percent) and Five (21 percent). Copper imports employed Routes Five (43 percent) and Three (33 percent). Thirty-four percent of Germany's lead supply and 29 percent of its zinc came over Route Five. In the case of bauxite, the principal trade routes were Four (twenty percent), Three (nineteen percent), and One (seventeen percent). All in all, the most important trade routes for crude oil are One and Two, while those for the metals are Five, Three, Four, Two, and One, respectively.

In the case of the United Kingdom, the most important trade routes, together with the percentages of supply carried over them in 1968 (1970 for crude oil), are as follows:

Crude oil—Routes Two (61 percent) and One (26 percent)

Iron ore—Routes Three (44 percent) and Five (18 percent)

Copper—Routes Five (49 percent) and Two (41 percent)

Lead—Routes Four (31 percent) and Five (22 percent)

Zinc—Routes Four (54 percent) and Five (23 percent)

Bauxite—Route One (22 percent)

In summary, the most important crude oil supply routes to the United Kingdom are Two and One. On the other hand, the most important shipping routes for the metals are, in descending order, Five, Four, Three, Two, and One.

TABLE 5

Percent of Total Supply of Selected Metals to Selected NATO
Countries Carried Over Different Sea Routes, 1968

Route Description	West Germany				
	Iron Ore	Cop-per	Lead	Zinc	Baux-ite
1. The Mediterranean	0.1	—	—	—	16.5
2. The Indian Ocean and the Eastern Atlantic (for exporting countries in South Asia, the Middle East, and East Africa)	0.4	—	—	—	—
3. The Eastern Atlantic, including the North Sea (for suppliers in West Africa and Scandinavia)					
Africa	18.7	33.0	4.6	0.8	18.7
Sweden and Norway	31.4	—	—	—	—
4. Across the Indian Ocean and the Eastern Atlantic (for suppliers located east of the Malacca Strait, such as Australia)					
Australia	2.8	—	1.5	0.2	20.2
Asia	1.2	—	0.9	—	—
5. Across the Atlantic (from countries in North and Latin America)					
North America	4.6	11.0	26.4	24.8	—
Latin America	16.7	32.5	7.8	4.0	4.8

	United Kingdom				
	Iron Ore	*Cop- per*	*Lead*	*Zinc*	*Baux- ite*
1. The Mediterranean	0.4	—	—	—	22.2
2. The Indian Ocean and the Eastern Atlantic (for exporting countries in South Asia, the Middle East, and East Africa)	0.1	40.9	—	—	5.4
3. The Eastern Atlantic, including the North Sea (for suppliers in West Africa and Scandinavia)					
Africa	26.6	—	3.2	—	—
Sweden and Norway	17.7	—	—	—	—
4. Across the Indian Ocean and the Eastern Atlantic (for suppliers located east of the Malacca Strait, such as Australia)					
Australia	0.8	—	30.9	54.2	—
Asia	—	—	—	—	—
5. Across the Atlantic (from countries in North and Latin America)					
North America	10.7	26.9	12.2	21.7	—
Latin America	7.2	22.9	9.7	1.3	6.3

France

	Iron Ore	Cop- per	Lead	Zinc	Baux- ite
1. The Mediterranean	0.2	—	24.2	16.1	2.0
2. The Indian Ocean and the Eastern Atlantic (for exporting countres in South Asia, the Middle East, and East Africa)	0.2	32.7	—	0.2	—
3. The Eastern Atlantic, including the North Sea (for suppliers in West Africa and Scandinavia)					
Africa	4.0	—	—	—	—
Sweden and Norway	0.5	—	—	—	—
4. Across the Indian Ocean and the Eastern Atlantic (for suppliers located east of the Malacca Strait, such as Australia)					
Australia	0.4	—	11.2	—	7.0
Asia	—	—	—	—	—
5. Across the Atlantic (from countries in North and Latin America)					
North America	—	14.1	1.7	18.0	—
Latin America	2.6	12.6	16.4	9.0	2.0

Source: Derived from Kimbell, *loc. cit.*

(Some small quantities undistributed by country of origin in the original data are omitted.)

TABLE 6

Percent of Total Supply of Crude Oil to Selected NATO Countries
Carried over Different Sea Routes, 1970

Route Description	*West Germany*	*United Kingdom*	*France*
1. The Mediterranean	48.0	26.2	43.4
2. The Indian Ocean and the Eastern Atlantic (for exporting countries in South Asia, the Middle East, and East Africa)	31.6	60.8	44.1
3. The Eastern Atlantic, including the North Sea (for suppliers in West Africa and Scandinavia)	6.8	7.5	6.4
4. Across the Indian Ocean and the Eastern Atlantic (for suppliers located east of the Malacca Strait, such as Australia)	—	—	—
5. Across the Atlantic (from countries in North and Latin America)	3.2	4.9	2.2

Source: Derived from *World Energy Supplies, 1961-1970*, UN Statistical Papers, Series J, no. 15 (New York: United Nations, 1972).

For France, the principal shipping routes are as follows:

Crude oil—Routes Two (44 percent) and One (43 percent)

Copper—Routes Two (33 percent) and Five (27 percent)

Lead—Routes One (24 percent), Five (18 percent), and Four (11 percent)

Zinc—Routes Five (27 percent) and One (16 percent)

Bauxite—Route Four (7 percent)

France is not significantly dependent on sea routes for iron ore supply, although some import comes from Algeria, the Scandinavian countries, and West Africa. Like the United Kingdom, France relies on Routes Two and One for its imported crude oil, and Routes Five, One, Four, and Two, in descending order, for metallic ores.

If we take these three major US allies together, their most important supply routes for petroleum clearly extend from the Indian Ocean around the Cape, and into the Eastern Atlantic. Second, the route across the Atlantic is most important for the supply of metals. Third, the route from South and West Africa is also important for metals, including uranium ore from South Africa. Fourth, as a source of the raw materials treated in this monograph, Australia is important especially to the United Kingdom. Finally, the Mediterranean is of importance primarily as an oil route from North Africa to West Germany, France, and other countries of Western Europe.

In dealing with raw material supply to Japan, we need to distinguish four additional sea routes: (6) the Asian waters east of the Malacca Strait; (7) across the Indian Ocean and through the Malacca Strait; (8) from the Eastern Atlantic (for West African suppliers) across the Indian Ocean and through the Malacca Strait; and (9) across the Pacific. Instead of going through the Malacca Strait, an alternative to Routes Seven and Eight is to go around Australia to Japan.

Table 7 provides detailed route information on individual imports. The principal trade routes and percent of total supply—for crude oil in 1970, and for metals in 1968—are as follows:

Crude oil—Routes Seven (85 percent) and Six (13 percent)

Iron ore—Routes Nine (32 percent), Six (26 percent), and Seven (17 percent)

Copper—Routes Seven (42 percent) and Nine (20 percent)

Lead—Routes Nine (34 percent) and Six (20 percent)

Zinc—Routes Nine (34 percent) and Six (12 percent)

Bauxite—Route Six (96 percent)

In summary, the most important trade routes for metallic ores, in descending order of importance, are Six, Nine, and Seven; the most important oil routes are Seven and Six. Thus, like Western Europe, Japan's oil supply is predicated upon security in the Indian Ocean. In addition, Japan is dependent upon free transit through the Malacca Strait and in the South and East China Seas. For metals supply, including uranium from Australia, the sea lanes east of the Malacca Strait are of primary importance. Finally, for metallic ores, including uranium from Canada and enriched uranium from the United States, the trans-Pacific route is vital.

As can be seen from Table 8, the United States is primarily interested in transportation between North and South America, including the Caribbean, as well as transit through the Panama Canal. In the longer run, if dependence upon Middle Eastern oil should increase, as is generally predicted, the significance of the Indian Ocean would rise.

TABLE 7

Percent of Total Supply of Crude Oil and Selected Metals to
Japan Carried Over Different Sea Routes, 1968

Route Description	Crude Oil*	Iron Ore	Cop-per	Lead	Zinc	Baux-ite
6. The Asian waters east of the Malacca Strait						
Australia	0.2	18.9	——	13.4	8.2	37.4
Indonesia	12.9	——	——	6.6**	4.2**	30.9
Other	——	7.0	——	——	——	28.0
7. Across the Indian Ocean and through the Malacca Strait	85.2	17.4	41.6	0.4	——	0.4
8. From the Eastern Atlantic (for West African suppliers) across the Indian Ocean and through the Malacca Strait	1.7	8.8	——	——	——	0.4
9. Across the Pacific						
North America	neg.	7.5	6.1	16.6	4.6	——
Latin America	0.3	24.9	13.7	17.5	29.0	2.3

Source: Derived from *World Energy Supplies, 1961-1970*, UN Statistical Papers, Series J, no. 15 (New York: United Nations,
1972).

*The data are for 1970.

**All Asia.

TABLE 8

Percent of Total Supply of Crude Oil and Selected Metals to the
United States Carried Over Different Sea Routes, 1968

Route Description	Crude Oil*	Iron Ore	Copper	Lead	Zinc	Bauxite
Across the Atlantic	1.0	2.7	4.5	0.2	2.8	20.8
Across the Pacific	0.6	—	—	4.5	0.2	—
Between the Americas	2.7	10.8	14.6	6.4	19.1	62.4
From the Indian Ocean	1.7	—	0.7	—	—	—

Source: Derived from *World Energy Supplies, 1961-1970*, UN Statistical Papers, Series J, no. 15 (New York: United Nations, 1972).

*The data are for 1970.

4

Security of Supply

Vulnerability at Sources of Supply

For both NATO and Japan, raw material imports could be disrupted because a few principal suppliers are potentially hostile to the West and under certain conditions could threaten either to shut off supply or to redirect it to other buyers. The first alternative is unlikely to happen over any extended period. Self-interest alone would be sufficient to preclude such "irrational acts" that are injurious to the exporting countries themselves. In the short run, however, ideological and political considerations could cause some of these countries to take measures that are economically inadvisable. They may even be induced by third parties to engage in such acts.

With this in mind, we can regard the following suppliers as potentially within this category: for West Germany: Zambia, Guinea, Peru, and Chile for the supply of copper; for the United Kingdom: again Zambia for copper; and for France: Chile for copper and Guyana for bauxite. In the Pacific, the supply of copper to Japan could become vulnerable to disruptions in Zambia, Chile, and Peru. The same is true for iron ore imports from Chile and Peru.

In the case of NATO's crude oil imports, disruption at source could occur in four anti-Western, more or less Soviet-oriented producing countries (Algeria, Egypt, Iraq, and Syria), and also in Libya, the domain of the militant though anti-Communist Colonel Qadhafi. Furthermore, the USSR supplies a fraction of crude oil to France and West Germany. Fortunately for Japan, all of its principal suppliers in the Middle East, as well as Indonesia, are either conservative Arab states or countries basically suspicious of the Soviet Union.

The exporting countries regarded as "vulnerable" are principally developing countries that are either under leftist governments, such as Chile and Peru, or that have had special relations with the Soviet Union or the PRC. For instance, Zambia is Peking-oriented; Egypt, Iraq, Syria, and Algeria are large Soviet military and economic aid recipients; Libya, though anti-Communist, is extremely militant in the Arab-Israeli conflict. More than any other Arab state, Libya is quite capable of taking action against countries deemed unduly friendly to Isreal. These threats at source should be considered in conjunction with the growing insecurity of the Mediterranean as a result of Soviet naval expansion in the area.

An asymmetry exists between NATO and Japan. While both are interested in the security of the Indian Ocean and the oil-producing countries of the Middle East, NATO is more vulnerable at some of its oil and metal sources than Japan. If NATO were to divert its oil purchases from Libya and the four "Soviet-oriented" Arab states, it would be able to free itself simultaneously from threats to its sea lanes in the Mediterranean. The Mediterranean, where the Soviet naval presence has increased so markedly, happens to be the principal route used by exports from the same unreliable sources of supply. Unfortunately, the same is not true for Japan, and its flexibility is therefore more limited. Switching sources of supply in the Middle East has no such advantage. Most imports to Japan from outside the Americas must use the same sea lanes south of Japan even if they do not pass through the Malacca Strait.

Vulnerability of the West's Oil Imports from "Friendly Countries" in the Middle East

Are the traditionally friendly sources of oil supply really secure? The Arab states of Oman, the Union of Arab Emirates, Bahrain, Qatar, and Kuwait have been targets of subversion by the Popular Front for the Liberation of Oman and the Arab Gulf (PFLOAG) for some time. Recently, the Shah of Iran is said to have become concerned about arms shipments entering the Gulf from the outside. The Libyans under Colonel Qadhafi are well-known financial supporters of radical causes. Both on their own and under Soviet prodding, the Iraqis have shown more than a passing interest in neighboring Abu Dhabi and Kuwait. To a large degree, the future of these oil-rich small states depends upon the policies and effectiveness of the Shah and King Faisal of Saudi Arabia, who share a common interest in regional stability and the continuation of traditional rule. However, both also have their own ambitions and quarrels with their neighbors (for example, Saudi Arabia with Abu Dhabi of the UAE, and Iran with the rulers of some adjacent small Arab states.) The continued brandishments of Arab extremists such as Qadhafi also make it necessary for countries like Saudi Arabia to heed the call for anti-Israeli and anti-American threats and actions under the slogan of Arab unity, at least from time to time. The internal and external instabilities lend themselves to exploitation by the USSR quite apart from the opportunities offered by the continuing conflict of Egypt and the militant Arab states with Israel, which has kept the eastern Mediterranean in turmoil for a quarter century. Thus, the oil supply routes to Western Europe are highly vulnerable.[19]

Even in the Western Hemisphere, security of sources of supply and lines of transportation can no longer be taken for granted even by the United States. Early in 1973, a number of Third World countries tried to pressure the United States to transfer to Panama

---

[19] In May 1970, guerrillas in Syria sabotaged the Trans-Arabian pipeline that carries oil from Saudi Arabia to the Mediterranean, and the Syrian government refused to allow repairs. The latest incident of sabotage occurred in April 1973, when an American-owned refinery at the Beirut end of the pipeline was set afire following an earlier Israeli raid on local Arab guerrilla headquarters.

"effective sovereignty" over the Panama Canal, forcing the US representative on the Security Council, John Scali, to veto a resolution urging speedier negotiations. Nationalization of US copper mines and the assets of the International Telephone and Telegraph Corporation by the Allende Administration in Chile presents another straw in the wind.

Countermeasures by NATO and Japan

For the principal European members of NATO, the vulnerability of their oil supply stems from (1) general instability in the Middle East, (2) heavy dependence on oil from the militant Arab states of the Maghrib, and (3) their consequent dependence on the security of sea lanes in the Mediterranean. The second and third vulnerabilities are the outcome of a deliberate shift of imports from the Middle East to Algeria and Libya after 1966. The shift was intended to diversify sources of supply and save on transportation costs. According to some calculations, four times as much tanker space was needed to bring oil to Western Europe from the Persian Gulf via the Cape of Good Hope as from North Africa or through the eastern Mediterranean.[20] Thus, economic considerations were responsible for exchanging one vulnerability for another.

In the long run, new discoveries in the North Sea offshore of Norway and the United Kingdom may provide a substantial alternative source of supply for Western Europe. According to British reports,[21] the large Ekofish Field in the Norway sector and the Forties and Auk Fields in the UK sector, as well as discoveries in the Shetland Islands, are prospectively large producers even by Middle Eastern standards. Estimates in 1971 have put the projected production for 1975 at 50 million metric tons of crude. For 1980, the estimated output is from 100 to 250 million tons. Thus, it may be possible eventually to replace some of the Mediterranean sources of supply.

---

[20] See *Strategic Survey 1970*, p. 69.
[21] *The Mining Journal, Annual Review, 1972* (London: 1972).

Fortunately for Western Europe, the North Sea discoveries are located in an area where, in the absence of general war, NATO naval forces will at least stand a chance of securing the supply routes. An equally viable case does not seem to exist for Japan. According to the 1972 revised estimate of its Atomic Energy Commission, Japan's growing demand for energy will require a total generating capacity of 174,430 megawatts in 1980 and 301,700 megawatts in 1990.[22] Of these totals, 63 percent in 1980 and 44 to fifty percent in 1990 will consist of thermo power, fueled primarily by oil. In view of this rising demand, Japan has sought to assure supply, first, by participating in the exploration and development of new oil resources, and more recently, by purchasing existing Western interests in developed fields. Japan has also tried to make direct purchases from oil-producing countries under long-term contracts. The wideranging search for oil can be seen from the accompanying map, which shows the locations of the overseas interests of Japanese oil companies as of April 1970. New expansion into other areas, including, for example, Zaire, has since been reported. Japan has also been active in developing overseas investments in metals production, especially in Indonesia and Australia.

In most instances, however, Japan's concern has been motivated by economic considerations. Besides, its desire to diversify sources of supply cannot alter geopolitical realities. Unlike the United Kingdom and West Germany, new resource discoveries closer to Japan are in areas under the direct control or potential influence of the Soviet Union and the PRC.

Soviet and PRC Policies

Economic preoccupations on the part of Western countries and Japan have given the Soviet Union an opportunity to offer lures for trade and investment. Discussions of the Joint Japan-Soviet Economic Committee since July 1966 have touched upon a number of potential projects under a production-sharing formula.[23] The first bilateral

---

[22] June 1972 "White Paper" of the Japanese Atomic Energy Commission.
[23] See Kiichi Saeki, "Toward Japanese Cooperation in Siberian Development," *Problems of Communism* (May-June 1972).

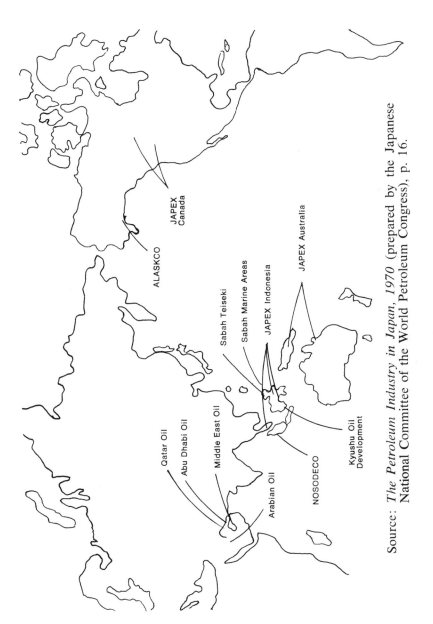

Source: *The Petroleum Industry in Japan, 1970* (prepared by the Japanese National Committee of the World Petroleum Congress), p. 16.

arrangement was a 1967 agreement to develop Soviet forest resources. Japan was to supply the USSR with materials for development and consumption over a three-year period in return for eight million cubic meters of timber. In addition, payments would be made by both sides for their respective imports. Subsequent negotiations have concerned the construction of a new harbor in the Bay of Wrangel, natural gas development in Sakhalin and in the Yakutskaia Autonomous SSR, and the supply of Soviet coal and iron ore to Japan. The Soviet Union has invited Japanese participation in the development of the Tyumen oilfields in West Siberia and the construction of a 6,660 kilometer pipeline from Anzhero-Sudzhensk to the port of Nakhodka. This pipeline project, proposed at the first session of the Joint Committee in March 1966, envisaged a Japanese credit of 1.45 billion rubles, with repayment of principal and interest through Soviet oil exports over a twenty-year period. Another early proposal, suggested by Japan but now in abeyance, was the development of the Utokan copper mine, six hundred kilometers to the northeast of Chita.

The North Sakhalin natural gas project and the copper mine proposal have so far come to naught. The Tyumen oil proposal, a prime Soviet target, also has not yet come to fruition. A common obstacle has been the very large demand for Japanese credit, combined with the insufficient technical and other information that the Soviet side has seen fit to supply. Furthermore, when the Tyumen oil project was proposed in 1966, the amount of Soviet oil exports to Japan envisaged was from ten to twelve million tons a year. Obviously, unless this figure can be raised substantially—more recent estimates have already raised the potential to 20-55 million tons—the net benefit that could accrue to Japan would be minimal in comparison to its overall requirements. The benefit scale is just not large enough to assure Japan of a closer source of substantial supply or to warrant the disproportionately large cost of investment.

In recent years, the governments of Japan, the Republic of China on Taiwan, and the Republic of Korea have handed out concessions for drilling rights on the continental shelf of the East China Sea, around the Korean Peninsula, and between the islands of Taiwan and Kyushu. Some of these activities were sparked by surveys carried out for the UN Economic Commission for Asia and the Far East in 1968 and 1969. While the initial grants of oil concessions were made without reference to Peking, the PRC has since suggested that Japan join it in a cooperative effort at offshore exploration. Since a major oil discovery has been made recently on the Shantung Peninsula, the PRC may have this particular area in mind. According to the *Nihon Keizai Shimbun* (April 18, 1973), the PRC has agreed to provide the Japan International Oil Company with one million tons of crude each year. The low sulphur oil is sold, however, at slightly above the world price.

The Soviet Union has good reasons to want Japanese economic cooperation. It is faced with (1) a rising demand for energy resources both at home and in Eastern Europe, (2) the fact that domestic production of some of these resources in established areas may not be as promising as has been estimated earlier, and (3) an urgent need, for economic as well as strategic reasons, to accelerate the development of Siberia and the Soviet Far East.[24] Abstracting for the moment from the very small oil exports from Tyumen promised to Japan in the original 1966 Soviet proposal, one could envisage a pattern of oil trade that would be greatly beneficial to the Soviet Union. Such a pattern would include the redirection of a major portion of Middle Eastern oil to the Soviet Union, either for the latter's own use or for reexport. This would be accompanied by a substantial increase in Soviet oil export to Japan, as well as to both Eastern and Western Europe. Such an arrangement would put both Japan and NATO at the mercy of Soviet policy. It would reinforce the already expanding influence of the Soviet Union over Middle Eastern countries, including those on both sides of the Red Sea, being effected through a substantial military aid program.

Until recently, such a fantastic rearrangement of the world's oil trade would have appeared too unrealistic. The Soviet Union has not been able to offer worldwide marketing, distribution, and other facilities sufficient to persuade even a producing country totally hostile

---

[24] "Le Potentiel Energétique de L'URSS, Perspectives 1975-1980." *Notes et Etudes Documentaires*, nos. 3926-3927 (Paris: La Documentation Francaise, 1972).

to the West to break relations with the large Western-owned international oil companies. A small Soviet breakthrough was made in Iraq when, following the nationalization of the Iraq Petroleum Company in June 1972, Soviet development aid to the Iraq National Oil Company was increased. The Soviet Union promised its help in distributing oil from the Kirkuk field (formerly IPC) and in bringing the North Rumaila field into large-scale production. According to a British report,[25] Iraq applied in October 1972 for observer status in COMECON, the Soviet-sponsored Council for Mutual Economic Assistance. The conclusion of the Soviet-Iraqi treaty in April 1972, and stepped-up Soviet arms shipments to Iraq, seemed to be part and parcel of the expansion of Soviet influence in the Middle East. While a radical redirection of the world's oil traffic seems beyond Soviet grasp for the present, the situation may be changing.

During the past ten years, members of the Organization of Petroleum Exporting Countries (OPEC) have been eminently successful in raising the price of oil and their share in royalties. From 1959 to 1969, partly as a result of increased demand and production, government oil revenue increased by 257 percent in Iran, 200 percent in Saudi Arabia, 100 percent in Kuwait, and 99 percent in Libya.[26] The trend is toward even greater increases in the future. Recent estimates have put future royalty receipts of the main oil-producing countries in the Middle East at tens of billions of dollars each year. As one contemplates the energy crisis, the usual question is how such large outpayments can be made and how they would affect the US balance of payments. Yet there is a distinct theoretical possibility that such large dollar payments will actually not have to be made, although the development leading to such a state of affairs would not be particularly welcome. For unless there is a radical improvement in the value of the US dollar and its international acceptability, the oil-producing countries may be unwilling to accept dollars in payment. They may develop a new incentive to redirect their oil exports, while the international oil companies may find themselves

---

[25] Strategic Survey 1972 (London: International Institute for Strategic Studies, 1973), p. 28.
[26] Strategic Survey 1970, p. 68.

no longer the commanding voice in such management decisions. At any rate, what the Soviet Union cannot accomplish by itself may have been made possible by US international economic misfortunes.

The Soviet Union must be prepared to face Chinese competition if it wishes to exercise its leverage on Japan through raw material supply. Oil is not the only mineral involved. Another key commodity could conceivably be uranium as fuel for Japan's reactors.

5

Strategic Issues on the Horizon

Rethinking Some Conventional Wisdom

The preceding discussion calls for some serious rethinking on a good deal of conventional wisdom. One hitherto generally accepted point is the proposition that the Suez Canal should be reopened. Since the Suez could not be reopened without agreement between Egypt and Israel, reopening would be symbolic of an Arab-Israeli detente, which is desirable *per se*. However, one needs to reexamine the exact net strategic advantage, if any, that the reopening of the Canal might produce. In the first place, the reopening of a shorter route for Middle Eastern oil to Western Europe could reduce transportation costs and economize time and tanker usage. But with the expansion of the international fleet of oversized tankers, economy of costs from the shorter route will no longer be as large as would have been the case ten years ago. Besides, the really large tankers

42

cannot pass through the Suez without substantial widening and dredging of the waterway.

The most fundamental question from the defense point of view is whether it pays to substitute for a longer route what may be a more vulnerable one. Unless the Mediterranean can be made really secure, does it pay to fall back on this waterway as the main highway of energy supply to Western Europe? As a matter of fact, one could even argue the opposite case, namely, that an attempt should be made to reduce NATO's dependence upon North African oil as long as the principal producing countries in the area are politically unstable and potentially hostile. Should French interest in Libyan oil be allowed to influence France to sell fighter aircraft to Libya? Should Western demand for Libyan oil be the factor that enables Qadhafi to offer financial support to various dissident groups in different parts of the world? These are typical questions requiring more careful examination by policymakers.

Another factor to be weighed in shortening the oil route by reopening Suez is that it provides a much more convenient passageway between the Black Sea and the Indian Ocean for the Soviet Navy. The optimists can perhaps argue that by reducing the length of the voyage that the Soviet fleet must now make from the Black Sea (or the Baltic) to the Indian Ocean (or its Pacific base), the demand for a larger Soviet fleet will be reduced so that the Soviet Union may decide to cut back its rate of naval expansion. A more pessimistic view, however, would not place too much confidence in this possibility. Instead, it would point to the greater ease with which the Soviet Union could build up its naval presence in the Indian Ocean to a desired level, and the greater mobility that Soviet vessels would then enjoy.[27]

A second point of conventional wisdom is the popular, usually implicit assumption that settlement of the Arab-Israeli dispute would resolve once and for all our concern about the Middle East. There is no doubt that the Arab-Israeli conflict is a potential cause of direct

---

[27] Against this Soviet advantage is the greater mobility that US vessels would also enjoy. Thus, a determining factor may be the relative rates of expansion of the two sides.

Soviet-US confrontation. On the other hand, it may not pay the Soviet Union to reduce Arab-Israeli tensions even though it may be against Soviet interest to have open war between them. Even if an agreement can be patched up between the two sides, we still cannot assume that a degree of stability will necessarily descend upon all the major oil-producing countries in the Middle East, whose internal tensions have been at least partly responsible for their external intransigence and, in some cases, downright truculence. A more fundamental solution must deal with the combined problems of (1) expanding the oil supply to meet growing demand, (2) increasing the rate of economic development and consumption of the Middle East, and (3) reconciling the national aspirations of the oil producing countries with the consuming countries' desire for international stability.

A third point is the conventional controversy surrounding proposals for developing US imports of Soviet natural gas and oil, together with US participation in developing Siberian and other Soviet resources. The usual controversy is between those who fear over-dependence on Soviet supply for security reasons, and those who hope for greater detente as a result of economic cooperation. It would seem that two significant points have generally been missed in popular discussions. First, how much control will each country have on its contribution to such schemes of cooperation, and to what degree are they irreversible by both sides? Second, what if the fears should become facts, or if the hopes are not realized? What provisions would be available, and would the other sides be aware of their existence, and therefore be more willing to continue cooperation? Above all, will the US public and its elected representatives understand the issues involved? If not, what can be done to enhance such understanding?

Areas of Neglect in US Policy

We turn next to certain areas of neglect in US policy. Until the recent devaluations of the dollar, the US government and the American public were apparently proceeding on the basis of the comforting assumption that the dollar would always be acceptable to foreign countries as something that people all over the world would be willing to accumulate indefinitely. We are now faced with the distinct possibility that some oil-producing countries may soon be acquiring annually such large sums of dollars that the US balance of international payments will have serious difficulty in making up the potential drain. Even then, the assumption still is that so long as the dollars are forthcoming, the oil-producing countries will be prepared to accept them. What if this assumption is not true? Would the exporting countries begin actively to look around for alternative, non-dollar markets? In such an event, the United States would face the serious possibility that some of its present allies would be forced to realign themselves in a manner detrimental to US interest.

Assuming that the United States does not find itself in such dire straits, and that the dollar retains its international acceptability and usefulness as a reserve currency. We must then face the threat to the balance of payments posed by the large oil revenues the producing countries will earn. What has been said about oil is equally applicable to other raw materials whose producers still accept dollar payments.

The potential problem posed by oil is basically a reflection of the general deterioration of the US balance of payments. This deterioration is itself a manifestation of our national tendency to live beyond our means, and to assume unquestioningly that this country's relative productivity will continue to rise faster than that of other countries— even though there is plentiful evidence to the contrary. Consequently, we may find ourselves forced by economic considerations to reduce our military presence in Europe, for example, and to be unable to respond to future challenges overseas even after the antiwar sentiments engendered by the Vietnam conflict have died down.

At the time of the Marshall Plan, few people would have imagined the possibility of a dollar glut only 25 years later. Future historians may find that the shift from a dollar shortage to a dollar glut has marked the end of an era. It does not mean that we should immediately swing from total complacency to total pessimism. But there is good reason to avoid imprudence and neglect, and to treat even the improbable and unthinkable as contingencies not to be lightly dismissed. One of these contingencies is the future attitude of important raw material suppliers—such as, for example, the nonferrous exporters of Latin America—toward their continuing relationship with the United States. Will Chile and Peru become even more anti-American than they have been in recent years? Will they be induced to reorient their foreign policy still further toward the Soviet Union and/or the PRC? Can we continue to assume that security of the Panama Canal itself will not be challenged in earnest?

These thoughts suggest that there should be a serious search for alternative sources of supply of the key raw materials that sustain the economies of the United States and its allies, as well as a major effort to find new methods of production employing substitute materials and alternative technologies. The controversial proposal of the trans-Alaskan pipeline and the policy to promote the expansion of nuclear power are only important examples of a much larger issue encompassing other materials and other technologies. The United States needs not only an energy policy, but also a raw materials policy in general. Domestic policies that fail to encourage innovative approaches or to provide against future threats to national security need to be reexamined more often than they seem to have been in the recent past.

Assuming for the moment that we do not face insuperable challenges to the supply of raw materials at the sources of supply or as a result of our inability to pay for them, there remains the issue of the security of trade routes. Threats to the security of sea transportation can occur (1) along littoral states close to the sea lanes, (2) at narrow passageways through which shipping must pass, and (3) from hostile air and naval threats in open waters. The littoral countries of the Indian Ocean, the West African states with access to Atlantic sea routes, the Malacca Strait, the Indonesian Sunda and Lombok Straits, and the insular Asian states (the Philippines and Taiwan) between Indonesia and Australia in the South, as well as Japan in the North, are all strategic positions to be safeguarded. Security of the main sea lanes requires not only the protection of shipping from these positions, but also their denial to potentially hostile powers. From a positive point of view, one needs to maintain both our own and our allies' access to important raw materials so that the present Atlantic and Pacific alliances can remain viable. From a negative point of view, one needs to deny to potential adversaries the positions from which they can exercise leverage to the detriment of the cohesion of the alliance system. Failure to accomplish both objectives could well jeopardize the grand design for a stable multipolar world. The strategic importance of the trans-Atlantic and trans-Pacific routes is well ingrained in American thinking. The British long ago recognized the vital role of the Cape route from the Middle East and across the Indian Ocean. But how many people realize the importance of Japan's lifelines in the Asian waters *to the United States*, or that the role of the Seventh Fleet does not cease with the Washington-Peking detente, because it is needed to insure the viability and reliability of the US-Japanese alliance, from the point of view of *both* countries?

The raw material-producing countries, especially the increasingly affluent oil producers, have an intrinsic interest in safeguarding their sources of external earnings and in putting these earnings to good use, toward the day when their present natural resources will become depleted. It is commonplace to suggest that these countries should use their oil earnings for economic development projects. The United States could pursue this matter with greater urgency, with a view to the oil-producing countries using their dollar receipts on development projects based on US exports. Beyond this, since there is a common interest between producing and consuming countries to safeguard the trade routes, it will behoove them to consider joint naval development for patrol and ASW purposes. This is a subject which conceivably could interest Japan. Could Japan and Indonesia, in view of the increasing share of the former's oil imports from the latter, be induced to make such an arrangement? Or Japan and Australia, if the latter's present policy under the Labor government should be modified? How about Japan and Iran? The basic principles of "Vietnamization" can be applied equally to other areas and other purposes. This is an approach going beyond the sale of Phantom jets to Saudi Arabia and Kuwait; it is a broader approach which can well encompass such sales, which have been reported in mid-1973.

What has been said of Middle Eastern oil and Latin American nonferrous metals in this monograph reflects certain long-term trends and potential conflicts of national interests that must be reconciled by careful design. From the point of view of the countries producing and exporting these resources, they are unwilling to remain simply as exporters of primary products. They want a larger share of the revenue; and they want to participate in, if not yet fully control, the management of the production and sale of their major resources and principal exports. The participation in and control of management which they envisage extend to the scale of exploitation of the resources in question—which are, after all, ultimately fixed in amount —and to the destination of these exports and the manner of their final sale to users in the importing countries. The last consideration points to a clear and, in fact, growing interest of the producing countries in the ownership and control of the processing and distribution stages of their primary exports. At the same time, the producing and exporting countries are profoundly interested in being able to maintain production and export; they would not wish to control production without an export market, since their own domestic consumption will continue to be only a negligible proportion of total production. Besides, once they have acquired investments in processing and distribution in certain export markets, they will have a vested interest in keeping those markets open. In such circumstances, they would not wish to have to redirect their export sales to other export markets where the existing distribution channels in which they have an interest do not function.

From the point of view of the consuming and importing countries, their interest is to safeguard an adequate supply that can be obtained at reasonable cost. Diversification of sources of supply and of import routes, long-term purchasing contracts at stable prices, participation in the development of the resources in return for guaranteed future deliveries, are the usual methods employed to achieve their basic purposes. At the same time, the importing countries would not wish to become overdependent on individual suppliers or routes of transportation; nor would they wish to incur an increasingly large burden on their balance of payments through these imports. Hence, they have a need to develop a market for their own exports that could

match the growing volume of these imports, possibly by tying investment and other assistance for the development of the primary exports
in the producing countries with broader development projects that
will demand their own exports in return. Other needs for imports,
apart from broad development needs, such as weapons imports for
defense and participation in international security arrangements,
would also fall into this category.

Lastly, from the point of view of countries that could provide
technical assistance and capital investment for the development of
raw material resources in the producing countries, their interest is the
profitability and security of their investments in addition to whatever
other national interest they may have *vis-à-vis* the producing and consuming countries. This category of investing countries and their
interests should be considered separately from the last two categories
—the exporting countries and the consumer countries. Although
many consuming countries invest in the development of these
resources, not all investing countries need to be net importing countries, especially of the exports of countries where they have in-
vested or provided development assistance. The United States, for
instance, is a large investing country in Middle Eastern oil, but was
not a large importing country of Middle Eastern oil in the past. As
one looks into the future, the United States may become an increasingly larger importing country of some of the resources discussed
in this monograph.

At the same time, the United States, as an investing country that
can help develop these resources, has definite strategic and other
interests in both major producing countries and their principal con-
sumers. (The Middle Eastern Arab states, Iran, certain Latin American countries, Canada, and Australia are among the countries in the
first group, while Japan and the principal European partners of
NATO are in the second group.) The principal task facing the
United States would seem to be the exercise of its role as an investing
country in a manner that would make the two sets of producing and
consuming countries anxious to cooperate with it in their own interest.
Participation in general economic development as well as in the development of specific resources, such as oil and uranium, in countries

that will be among the major suppliers of the consuming countries, and the creation of closer economic ties between the producing countries and the American market so that they cannot be easily broken off, appear to provide the general framework within which detailed schemes might be worked out. This approach should be integrated with attempts to increase cooperation between foreign producing and consuming countries, such as Japan and Iran. The raw material problem facing the United States, of which the energy crisis is but an example, is more than simply the need to balance an increasing demand against a supply that we can afford.

In conclusion, we should remind ourselves that external security requires a compatible domestic policy, and an appropriate mechanism and the personnel to coordinate the two. Just as we must not neglect domestic priorities in formulating defense policy, so we must consider the cost to defense in pursuing domestic concerns. Externally, the United States faces the danger of drifting progressively into a position from which it will not be able to exercise influence at any great distance from its own shores. Such an outcome is by no means inevitable if the trends are perceived and corrective measures taken in time. Perhaps the review of the raw material situation in this monograph will serve the purpose of sounding a warning on a much wider scale.

Suggested Readings

Relatively little has been published in the last few years on the strategic aspect of raw material supply. The following selections will, however, provide the basic background information for further study.

Atomic Energy Commission, Japan, *General Review of the Long Term Program of the Development and the Utilization of Atomic Energy* (Tokyo: 1972).

Bureau of Mines, US Department of the Interior, *Minerals Yearbook*, 1969 and subsequent years, especially the section on international trade and foreign production and consumption.

Melvin A. Conant, "Oil, Cooperation or Conflict," *Survival*, vol. 15, no. 1 (January-February 1973).

Richard Ellingsworth, *Japanese Economic Policies and Security*, Adelphi Papers No. 90 (London: International Institute for Strategic Studies, 1972).

Frank L. Fisher, *A Classification of Metals: Their Etymology and Functional Groupings* (Washington: Bureau of Mines, October 1965).

Japan External Trade Organization, "The Actual Situation of Japanese Foreign Investments: White Paper on *Overseas Markets*" (Tokyo: August 1972). Summary given in JETRO, *Trade and Industry in Japan*, vol. 21, no. 8 (November 1972).

Wilfred Malenbaum, *Materials Requirements in the United States and Europe in the Year 2000* (Washington: National Commission on Materials Policy, 1973).

Organization for Economic Cooperation and Development, *Energy Policy* (July 1966).

_____. *The Search for and Exploitation of Crude Oil and Natural Gas in the European Area of OECD* (October 1962).

————. *Uranium* (September 1970).

————. *The Non-Ferrous Metals Industry, 1971* (November 1972).

————. *The Engineering Industries in OECD Member Countries, Basic Statistics, 1963-1970* (December 1972).

————. *Oil Statistics, 1971* (December 1972).

————. *Investing in Developing Countries* (October 1972).

————. *Foreign Trade Statistics*, Series A, B, and C on overall trade, regional data, and detailed analysis by products.

————. *Provisional Oil Statistics*, quarterly.

Strategic Survey 1970 (London: Institute for Strategic Studies, 1971), section on "Economic Policies and Security;" and *Strategic Survey 1972* (London: International Institute for Strategic Studies, 1973), section on "Oil and Policy in the Middle East."

Raw Material Supply in a Multipolar World by Yuan-li Wu, October 1973

The People's Liberation Army: Communist China's Armed Forces by Angus M. Fraser, August 1973

Nuclear Weapons and the Atlantic Alliance by Wynfred Joshua, May 1973

How to Think About Arms Control and Disarmament by James E. Dougherty, May 1973

The Military Indoctrination of Soviet Youth by Leon Gouré, January 1973

The Asian Alliance: Japan and United States Policy by Franz Michael and Gaston J. Sigur, October 1972

Iran, The Arabian Peninsula, and the Indian Ocean by R. M. Burrell and Alvin J. Cottrell, September 1972

Soviet Naval Power: Challenge for the 1970s by Norman Polmar, April 1972

How Can We Negotiate with the Communists? by Gerald L. Steibel, March 1972

Soviet Political Warfare Techniques, Espionage and Propaganda in the 1970s by Lyman B. Kirkpatrick, Jr., and Howland H. Sargeant, January 1972

53

54

The Soviet Presence in the Eastern Mediterranean by Lawrence L. Whitten, September 1971

The Military Un*balance*
  Is the U.S. Becoming a Second-Class Power? June 1971

The Future of South Vietnam by Brigadier F. P. Serong, February 1971 (Out of print)

Strategy and National Interests: Reflections for the Future by Bernard Brodie, January 1971

The Mekong River: A Challenge in Peaceful Development for Southeast Asia by Eugene R. Black, December 1970

Problems of Strategy in the Pacific and Indian Oceans by George G. Thomson, October 1970

Soviet Penetration into the Middle East by Wynfred Joshua, July 1970. Revised edition, October 1971

Australian Security Policies and Problems by Justus M. van der Kroef, May 1970

Detente: Dilemma or Disaster? by Gerald L. Steibel, July 1969

The Prudent Case for Safeguard by William R. Kintner, June 1969

Forthcoming

The Horn of Africa by J. Bowyer Bell, Jr.

On Research and Development and the Prospects for International Security by Frederick Seitz and Rodney W. Nichols

The Soviet Presence in Latin America by James D. Theberge

The Development of Strategic Weapons by Norman Polmar

Contemporary Soviet Defense Policy by Benjamin S. Lambeth